ME ON THE MAP

by Joan Sweeney   illustrated by Annette Cable

Dragonfly Books —🪰 New York

For Peggy, John, and Tom—J.S.

To the people who put me on the map,
Mom and Dad—A.C.

Text copyright © 1996 by Joan Sweeney
Illustrations copyright © 1996 by Annette Cable

Dragonfly Books with the colophon is a registered trademark of Random House, Inc.

Visit us on the Web! www.randomhouse.com/kids

Educators and librarians, for a variety of teaching tools, visit us at
www.randomhouse.com/teachers

Library of Congress Cataloging-in-Publication Data
Sweeney, Joan.
Me on the map / by Joan Sweeney ; illustrated by Annette Cable.
p.   cm.
Summary: A child describes how her room, her house, her town, her state, and her country
become part of a map of her world.
ISBN 978-0-517-70095-2 (trade) — ISBN 978-0-517-70096-9 (lib. bdg.) — ISBN 978-0-517-88557-4 (pbk.)
1. Maps—Juvenile literature. [1. Maps.] I. Cable, Annette, ill. II. Title.
GA130.S885   1996   912'.014—dc20   95014963

MANUFACTURED IN CHINA

35 34 33 32 31

This is me.

This is me in my room.

This is a map of my room.

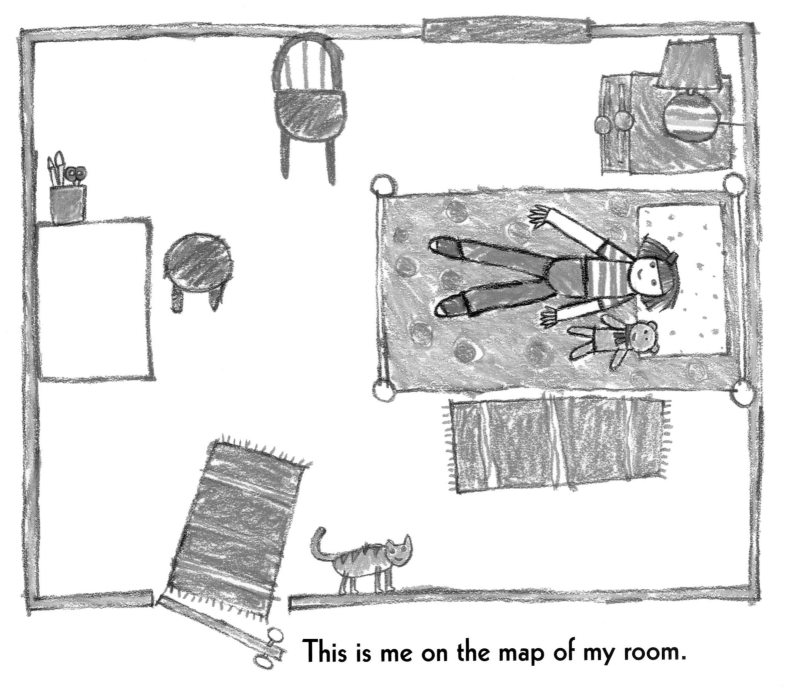

This is me on the map of my room.

This is my house.

This is a map of my house.
This is my room on the map of my house.

This is my street.

This is a map of my street.
This is my house on the map of my street.

This is my town.

This is a map of my town.

This is my street on the map of my town.

This is my state.

This is a map of my state.

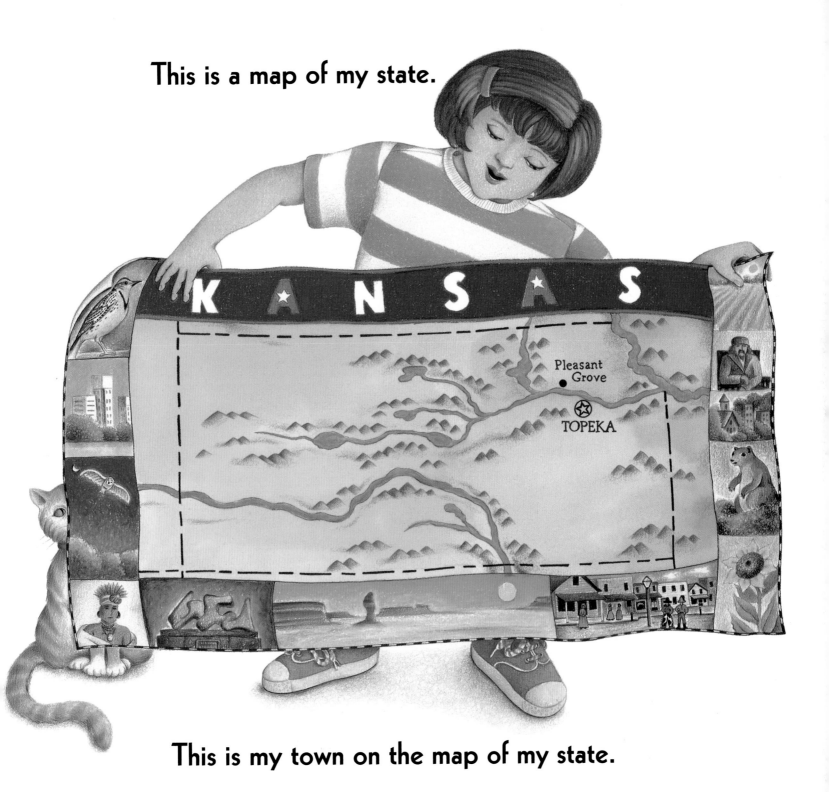

This is my town on the map of my state.

This is my country. The United States of America.

This is a map of my country.

UNITED STATES OF AMERICA

WASHINGTON
OREGON
MONTANA
IDAHO
NORTH DAKOTA
SOUTH DAKOTA
WYOMING
MINNESOTA
WISCONSIN
MICHIGAN
NEW HAMPSHIRE
VERMONT
MAINE
MASSACHUSETTS
NEW YORK
RHODE ISLAND
CONNECTICUT
NEW JERSEY
DELAWARE
MARYLAND
CALIFORNIA
NEVADA
UTAH
COLORADO
NEBRASKA
IOWA
ILLINOIS
INDIANA
OHIO
PENNSYLVANIA
WEST VIRGINIA
VIRGINIA
KANSAS
MISSOURI
KENTUCKY
NORTH CAROLINA
ARIZONA
NEW MEXICO
OKLAHOMA
ARKANSAS
TENNESSEE
SOUTH CAROLINA
MISSISSIPPI
ALABAMA
GEORGIA
TEXAS
LOUISIANA
FLORIDA
ALASKA
HAWAII

N
W
E
S

This is my state on the map of my country.

This is my world. It is called Earth.
It looks like a giant ball.

If you could unroll the world and make it flat...

...it would look something like this map of the world.

This is my country on the map of the world.

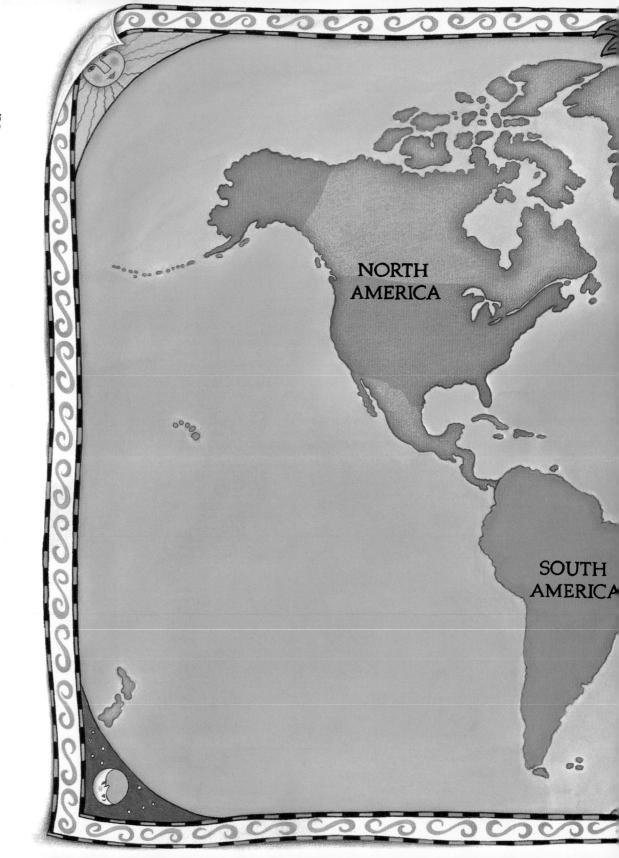

NORTH
AMERICA

SOUTH
AMERICA

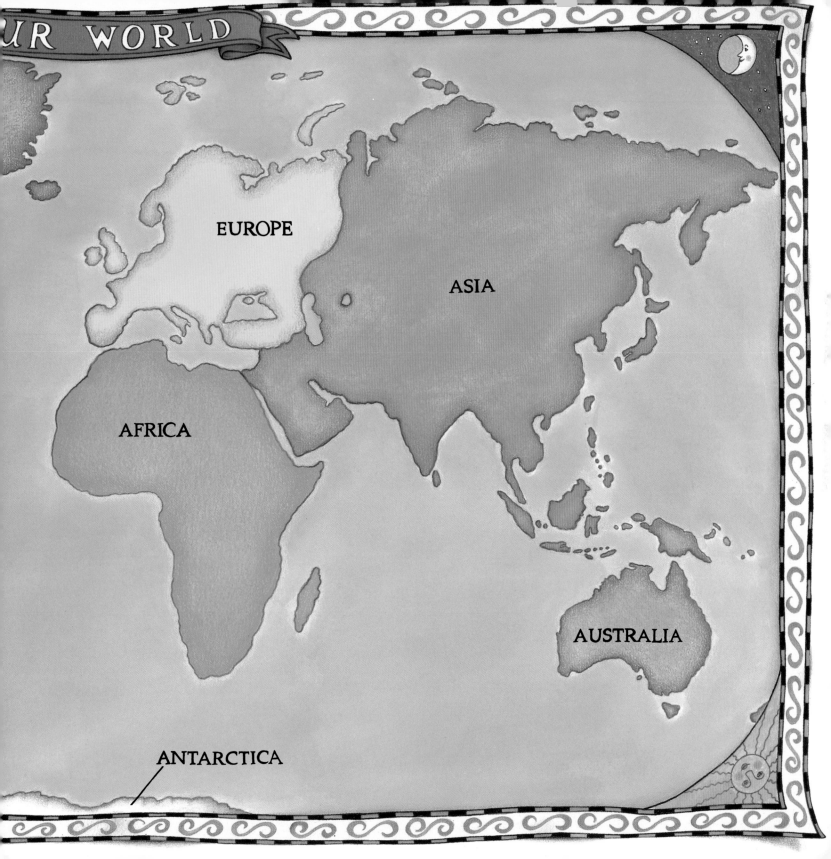

So here's how I find my special place on the map. First I look at the map of the world and find my country.

Then I look at the map of my country and find my state.
Then I look at the map of my state and find my town.

Then I look at the map of my town and find my street.

And on my street I find my house.

And in my house
I find my room.

And in my room I find me!
Just think...

...in rooms, in houses, on streets,
in towns, in countries all over the world,
everybody has their own
special place on the map.

Just like me.

Just like me on the map.

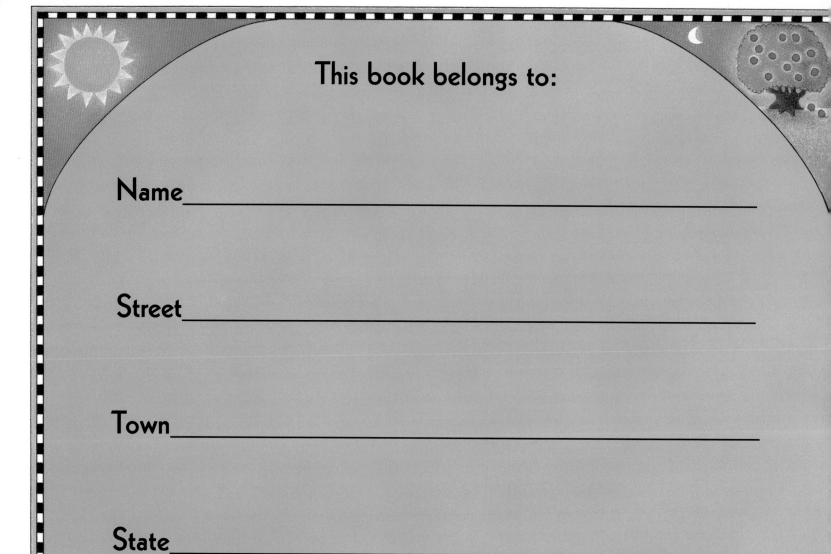

This book belongs to:

Name_____

Street_____

Town_____

State_____

Country_____